LEAVING A SHADOW

THE NATIONAL POETRY SERIES

The National Poetry Series was established in 1978 to publish five collections of poetry annually through five participating publishers. The manuscripts are selected by five poets of national reputation. Publication is funded by James A. Michener, the Copernicus Society of America, Edward J. Piszek, the Lannan Foundation, the National Endowment for the Arts, and the Tiny Tiger Foundation.

1995 COMPETITION WINNERS

Heather Allen, *Leaving a Shadow*
Selected by Denise Levertov, published by Copper Canyon Press

Marcus Cafagna, *The Broken World*
Selected by Yusef Komunyakaa, published by the University of Illinois Press

Daniel Hall, *Strange Relation*
Selected by Mark Doty, published by Viking Penguin Press

Juliana Spahr, *Response*
Selected by Lyn Hejinian, published by Sun & Moon Press

Karen Volkman, *Crash's Law*
Selected by Heather McHugh, published by W. W. Norton

THE NATIONAL POETRY SERIES
SELECTED BY DENISE LEVERTOV

HEATHER ALLEN

Leaving a Shadow

COPPER CANYON PRESS

Publication of this book is supported by a grant from the National Endowment for the Arts and a grant from the Lannan Foundation. Additional support to Copper Canyon Press has been provided by the Andrew W. Mellon Foundation, the Lila Wallace–Reader's Digest Fund, and the Washington State Arts Commission. Copper Canyon Press is in residence with Centrum at Fort Worden State Park.

Library of Congress Cataloging-in-Publication Data
Allen, Heather, 1953–
Leaving a shadow / by Heather Allen
   p.   cm.
ISBN 1-55659-113-6 (pbk.)
I. Title.
PS3551.L39276L43 1996
811´.54 – dc20   96-25195

COPPER CANYON PRESS
P.O. BOX 271, PORT TOWNSEND, WASHINGTON 98368

ACKNOWLEDGMENTS

"Walking with My Father" first appeared in the *New England
   Review*.
"The Cartographers" in *The Georgia Review*.
"The Country of Childhood" and "Dream Cycle" in *Poetry*.

For my parents

Contents

LEAVING A SHADOW

IN THE FOREST

Your step at once
More silent and more resonant,
Unmoving trees close ranks around you.
Darkness is suddenly deeper,
The web of light more clear.

Unseen the many eyes
That follow you, of sentinels
Stationed just beyond the rim
Of the senses, who merge into leaves and stillness
Just as you turn.

Shadow and substance, trees and light
Are finely braided here,
And passages to interwoven worlds
Are everywhere:
A flash of wings

From deep within
The coiled circuits of the leaves,
The grey hush of the goshawk
Gliding suddenly from the weave,
Or a placeless echo of the owl's dream.

Like the cipher
Of a still impenetrable text,
Tracks mark the fragment of a path
Along the boundary of dawn
Or a night's hunting,

Into a world old maps describe
Only as "Forest," "Unexplored."
Composed and watchful, the trees
Surround a trove of secret lives
That seem unreachable to us –

Concentric rings
Of deer in the clearings, the phantom lynx
Poised in the dark eye of a pool,
The deep and humid dens
Of fox and owl,

And surreptitious, snaking roots that hold
The forest in miniature –
Spiral ferns and intricately threaded mosses,
The strands, invisible in shadow,
Of the spider's lair.

There, a drift of feathers
Cast up by the throes of night
Echoes a bird's last cry,
In the grip of something
Stealthy, huge-eyed, a darkness

Shaped by scent, and hearing
Tuned to the faintest heartbeat –
The slow, implacable pulse
Of the hunter,
The wild throbbing of his prey.

Dense with portents,
It is a labyrinth

Of furtive curves
And endless branching,
Barrier and entrance –

Still, as it is for the hero
In the forest of dream and legend
A place of trials and revelation.
You go there alone.
You must find your own way in.

POOL

In a wide and quiet hollow
Where the river slows,
Dark in the shadow of the trees
And amber with the light of stones,

The water turns upon itself, and shifts
Transparent panes above an unknown depth.
Trees overhang
Their images, that seem to rest

Upon the dark leaves on the bottom,
Where twigs and spotted shadows
Turn to fish, and drift
Into the center of the pool to feed –

Their circles widening
Then disappearing,
Like echoes of a sound
Beyond our hearing.

DEER

Despite the mute conspiracy
Of trees and field,
The leaves and grasses that deny their passing,
They are here –

Tracks left at dawn, shadows
In an evening field.

The grove
Draws close around a secret clearing,
Bodies dappled in the light
Of inner leaves –

Hidden in the still
And luminous stand of winter rye,
There is a beating heart,
A dark and watchful eye.

FISH

Morning, and the light above the lake
Joins that below:
Unbroken calm.

Fish scatter from my shadow,
Then drift back again,
Taking their places with a deft
And magical cohesion.

In stillness held
To unseen moorings,
They hang suspended in a wheel
Of subtly undulating tiers,

A quiver of sentinels
Feeling the water's pulse,
Ready to fly in an instant.

GRASSES

So still at heart,
They respond like water
To the slightest breeze,
Rippling as one body,

And, as one mind,
Bend continually
To listen:
The perfect confidants,

They keep to themselves
A web of trails and nests,
Burrows and hidden entrances –
Do not reveal

Those camouflaged in stillness
From the circling hawks,
Or crouched and breathless
At the passing of the fox.

FISHERMEN

a Black trees that set
b Their nets in fog, its waters
c Rising to their knees,

a And catch in a smoky mesh
d Of branches
c A school of yellow leaves.

DAWN

The heron wakes
Within the spreading rings of dream,

As the last fish flash into the shadows
Of floating trees.

He fills his quiver, and without a sound
Glides off to his transparent hunting grounds.

DUSK

Now from the amber grove,
The field on fire,
Light turns away –
A shoal beneath which

Shadows rise,
Lengthen, and start to merge,
As the dark that was asleep
Begins to stir.

A line of single trees
Is carved out like a frieze against the sky,
Where day and night will balance
For a moment more

Before the last light
Finally yields,
And the owl
Swings out over the field.

CROW

So unhurried in its ways,
Yet when in an empty tree the crow
Alights and stays,
Its flight persists:

A germ of night
In a cloudless sky,
A wing that goes on beating
In the dark of the eye.

HILLS

At dusk, dreams interweave,
As flocks of shadows
Settle in the leaves

And a few clouds still remember light,
A faint and far-flung archipelago, the lake
Its last island.

From my canoe, the water's reverie,
Adrift between the shores
Of sleep and waking,

The hills around the lake appear
As folds and fissures in a brain
Of dense, incessant trees,

Their thoughts the swallows
That design a labyrinth
In the darkening air.

Along those shifting pathways where the mind
Seeks out the visions
Worthy of a dream,

Tonight the hills and I
Will fix on that circle
Of lake, trees, sky,

And a canoe
Balanced in the mirror
Of the mind's eye.

HERON

A master archer
Whose body is both
The arrow and the bow,

He watches without watching,
Undivided and at rest within –
Draws imperceptibly,

And finds his mark
In a fish's furtive gleam,
Its slightest shadow.

NIGHT IN THE MOUNTAINS

Gradually along the range
All things exchange their light
For darkness.

Single oaks
On hills that burned with gold
Merge now in shadow,

And hawks sail out
Over the valley,
Its air like a mirror

Filling with night,
That takes our images
And does not return them,

Just as the pines
Blot out our voices,
And even the stones at our feet

Fade from sight.
Now only the stars
Have eyes,

And around us sounds
Of things we cannot see
Begin to rise:

The owl's single note,
And the coyote's cry.

DREAM CYCLE

Out in the deep and sentient night,
A great slow pulse and breathing –
All boundaries dissolved,
The very dark is dreaming:

The heron wrapped in a thick cocoon of calm,
A long, lingering dawn in which
Shoal on shoal of lightfish
Fly within reach;

The fish themselves
In their own dream escaping –
Charmed by their winged reflection,
The shimmer of transparent leaves,

They rise suddenly into the trees'
Dense cloud of shadow.
There, in some far recess of sleep
The heartwood feels a trembling

Along the web of limbs, some sound…
The owl's cry
Spreading in concentric rings
In the wide eye of darkness,

While in the owl's dream he glides unheard,
Unseen above a field
Of soft, absorbent pitch, catacombed
With clear paths of sound,

And scattered with the gleam
Of scurried heartbeats.
Woven in the grasses, heavy with dew,
Are the spectral paths of deer

Asleep in the hushed
Sanctuary of the forest,
Where they wander unpursued,
Perfectly in tune

With groves of tawny light,
Invisible in thickets of stillness.
They are a dream the forest
Half remembers, a sense of something

Wild and seldom seen,
That fades so swiftly
Into the trees, and leaves no tracks
In the soft ground of waking.

Poised in the shrouded branches
Of a fogbound, uncanny calm,
The pale and princely goshawk
Surveys his realm –

A shifting, intricate terrain
Of treetops, coiling streams,
The cloak of forest opening
On luminous, secluded fields

And closing on the hills
In deep, slow drifts of shadow

That come to rest
Just at the edge of the lake,

The last trees leaning
Out over the water,
Rapt in a dream of floating.
The heron circles in to shore, stands listening

As night shifts in its sleep:
The darkness all alive
With many souls,
A single dreaming mind.

*

THE COUNTRY OF CHILDHOOD

Je suis de mon enfance comme d'un pays.
– ANTOINE DE SAINT-EXUPÉRY

Dawn in that country is a time
When the heron and the hills preside
Over the lake and its lingering dreams –
The fish, the folded water lilies, and the trees
That gradually retrace their leaves
In the water's mirror.
There, reflections and receding dreams
Share a shifting boundary

And mark, like the tracks left on the shore,
The threshold between two worlds.
Signs of secret lives
Spent in the dark,
Some are indecipherable, among
The raccoon's delicate handprints
And the birds' cuneiform,
Text of a lost tongue.

On the far shore, the hills
Contemplate the water's other range,
With its own white boathouse and passing birds,
A realm erased by the rising breeze.
The mist retreats from lake and trees,
A dwindling signal sent from other times –
From a sleeping swamp, or Indian fires
Still bright in a circle of stones.

Raised by the wind, schools of silver
Gather on the lake, then scatter,
Pursued by sails and swallows.
Light grows, collected in a web of leaves,
And deepens, beneath the trees,
The mossy caves of shadow.
Butterflies, the brightly colored
Fragments of a dream,

Settle in the garden,
Their wings a map of distant coastlines
And interiors still unexplored.
Birds find their way with ease
In a shifting maze of passages
Among the leaves,
Following the threads that lead
To hidden chambers –

A path into impenetrable trees
Where a shaft of light
Falls in the forest,
A door left ajar,
Or a wide, slow river
Flowing toward that brightness
Beyond the bend
Where the kingfisher and the heron go.

Toward dusk, the trees converge
In shadow and grow still,
As the birds withdraw into their secret bowers,
And a few lights shine on the hills.
Fish rise in circle after circle
As if an unseen rain were falling,

And bats emerge to map
The darkness with their cries.

Wild geese, preceded by a distant calling,
Show up briefly in the last light of the sky,
Then disappear as they descend
Against the shadow of the hills
And settle on the lake,
Only their voices visible.
Night deepens, listening for the owl,
And there are few familiar landmarks now –

No chart but stars,
As darkness yields to dream
And the trees go walking on a windy shore.
Birds dream of a labyrinth,
The hills of silent hunters,
And the water of their canoes.
The heron's dreams are lit by fish,
The lake's by the great pale marshes of the moon.

THE LAKE

Not lost, the stars
These hills are –
Their lines the boundless contour
Of an ancient mind,
Unfettered, dreaming, wild,

Encircling the lake, the first mirror
I looked into as a child.
There, light pervades a weightless world,
Where buoyant fishes balance perfectly above
A school of slender shadows,

So like the birds that fly among
The doubled hills and deep, transparent trees.
Poised intently as the heron,
The trees, too, are archers standing watch
Along the shore,

Guardians of memory, and of the hidden lives
That emerge with darkness,
Night hunters and the errant souls of dreams.
Above, the moon
Is an enigmatic target,

Its path on the water
Deceptively clear,
As the houselights on the hills are drawn
Into the net of gems
Cast by the stars.

The heavens are here:
In the secret lives
Of trees and water,
The shape of hills, each one
Patterned on a star –

And in the lake,
Like the polished mirror
At the heart of a shrine,
That stands for brightness
And the calm, untrammelled mind.

SAILBOAT

Strange flight, the body
Held at a threshold
And never quite freed

Or quite revealed –
One wing taut with wind,
One wing concealed

Until the wind grows calm
And it shimmers in a shadow-world,
The shape of a sail, yet softer –

The drifting boat
A bird half in air,
Half in water.

CANOE

Balance on the threshold of the lake
Like a fish suspended
On its nest of light,

And leave no tracks here
At the rim of another world.

Glide in beneath enchanted trees
That bend intently
To their studies –

The enigma of the dark, inverted birds,
Or the wind's next move
In the game of sun and shadow.

Offshore, the sandy shallows
Are a shifting glass
Reflecting things beyond us –

Where the mime of underwater weeds
Mirrors a slight wind
Far above in trees,

And clouds and fishes drift
Among transparent leaves.

WALKING WITH MY FATHER

Somewhere, we're still following
Where those old cut rows of corn
Were leading,
And as we walk, flushing
Dark birds up
From their feeding.

It's cold: our breath
Invents a body in the air.
Your hand hangs
Just at the level of my hair.
Above our heads, a crow is beating black
Against the light:

But night
Will never reach us there.
Ahead of us,
The dark trees always yield:
We'll never reach the end
Of that field.

JAPANESE LANTERNS

The lights of moth, firefly,
Moon, garden,
The deep white heart of the lotus

And the lake at dawn,
Where the boat of a single fisherman
Is doubled in the calm:

Still radiant in summer trees,
The lanterns of childhood –
To be carried always.

CROSSING OVER

For my father

Gradually the body
Grows less dense,
Becomes, like trees at night,
A darker shadow in the dark,
The wind a dream
Whose only image
Is the sound of leaves.

Time slows, and turns,
Like a pool, in quiet circles.
In that still, transparent medium
You slip without friction
Into the past –
The mind begins to move
From light to shadow,
Trees overarching the path.

Memory picks summer
As its season,
And we're riding in the woods again,
The road unwinding
Through a labyrinth of light and leaves,
Down into a darkened gully
Where we cross a stream,
And up into the clear –
The soft, noontime glare of a field,
Its life all hidden or asleep –
The timid shadows of the owl and the deer
Waiting for the camouflage of evening.

Now, too late to turn
Back toward this world,
The body is becalmed –
A sailboat on the lake,
One tall white wing
Looking in the water
For its twin, and a small
Dark figure listening –
Leaning toward a radiance
Still indistinct, a distant music:
Birds, voices, the whispered words
Of water to the shore at night.

That night
When sleep, with a single breath
Passed into death,
You had already gone
To another place,
Where a soft, smoky dawn
Polishes the surface of the lake,
Leaving it clear and calm,
And the horses walk toward us down the long
Field, in a light
Only glimpsed before –

That transparency
Where nothing well-loved
Ever disappears,
And time does not pass,
But only deepens –
Immobile, undiminished,
And almost clear.

LEAVING A SHADOW

From a still place
On the shore of the lake,
I look into the landscape
Of the soul –
A web of radiance, its heart
The child of summer
Drawn deep into the mirror of water

To swim with birds and fish
In the same luminous currents,
And drift into a veil of trees
As real as their reflections
In the branching shadows above us.
Here at the center
Of transparent time and space

Morning and evening
Circle in place,
Turning through haze and mist
Into the wind's dancing brilliance,
The liquid amber of late afternoon,
And the last islands of brightness
On the hills at dusk –

These hills encircling the lake
That have given me their shelter and their shape –
The hollows where smoke and shadows gather,
The long light-soaked slopes
Of the fields:
The clouds of forest
Dreaming in me still.

*

THE CARTOGRAPHERS

Haunted by an offshore wind,
A radiance just out of reach, the horizon
Like the threshold of an open door,
The known cannot hold them.

In the field they hear
The swiftly beating hearts of birds,
And feel the deer's dark eye –
Watch the wind's path
Sink in the tall grass,
And the thread the birds unwind
At the limit of sight.

In a circle of trees
Facing outward, bodies linked
More closely to defend
The secret clearing,

There is a maze where light and leaves
Have equal body, and the birds
Disappear into bowers of air,
Sharp and swift as yearning.

To see how solid things are shadowed
By a luminous transparency
Is to discover
How this world maps another –

It is for their art to show
The shape the birds design, their spiral flight

The subtle circling of fate,
The twists of time;

To draw the bodiless and shifting trees
That live in a quiet pool,
And render its deceptive clarity, its light
The light of memory –

Where scenes of deepening brilliance rest
Like the bright stones on the bottom,
Out of reach.

Just how far away
That brightness is
No map can show –
Its art can bring us only to the edge

Of the secret center
In the labyrinth of trees,
The paths that die out
In the forest, mountains, sea –

The unyielding distance
Cartographers call
Strange beauty.

BIRDS

Arrows released
From an unseen bow,
Birds aim unerringly
For the heart of the trees –
Alight, and balance instantly.

Within the maze
Of sun and shadow,
They thread their way through spiral passages
That link two worlds,
And from the radiance that is their home

They bring back messages in a forgotten code –
Few augurs now
To read the future in their flight,
Or trace celestial patterns
In the fading light.

As dusk delivers trees and hills
From their fixed shape,
The birds are hidden voices in a dark
And fluid landscape, their last calls
Especially clear, as if carried over water

From the realm
They would reveal –
Where spirit has more substance
Than flesh and bone,
And the body is a shadow
Cast by the soul.

WIND

As clouds close swiftly
Over the sun, the horses in the field
Start up, and run –

The water of the pond
Goes dark, disturbed by tracks
That spark

Then disappear,
And the slender reeds
Are thrust away, as if

From a powerful body:
Unseen, known only
By the feel of its breath –

By troubled horses,
Tracks on darkened water,
Reeds that point to its path.

CLOUD SHADOWS

Just as my own thoughts
Drift across the hills,
Savoring the soft clefts
Where slopes converge,
And trying to infiltrate
The closely-woven leaves
Of forest deep in its own brooding,

So too another mind
Moves in the shifting shapes of cloud and sun.
A flowing brightness
Feels for hidden openings, is overcome
By slow-encroaching shadow,
Then seeps back again –
To linger in the hollows
And, perhaps, to fathom
The impenetrable trees.

MOON WATCH

The dense and secret hills
Withdraw in mystery,
The forest folded in upon itself –

Suspended in a dream, the trees
Dissolve into their shadows,
A cloud of dark, still leaves.

Across the lake, a ladder of light
To a far-off swath of eerie
Insubstantial silver,

And above, the radiant sphere –
Mirror of the ancient mind
That is called and answers instantly:
Serene, unimpeded, clear.

HELIOTROPE

How pliant the body
When the sun
Suddenly appears –
Each cell turning as one

Like the gleaming shoal
Or swift-spiralling cloud
Of birds and fish
Moving in unison.

How every leaf and stem
Lifts upward,
Drawn to the light,
And every petal opens –

The flower's deepest heart
Thirsty for radiance,
And beating now
With the same slow pulse as the sun.

How, once suffused with heat
And luminous, each cell
At dusk yearns for noon –
In the darkness, remembers you.

SLEEP

A swell of shadows
Slowly carries
The soul from the body,
A ship launched on the darkness toward
The threshold of an undiscovered shore –

By no light
But the light of your skin,
Hands I cannot see
Unfurl its sail: a whiteness
That your breathing catches in.

THE SHAPE OF FATE

In the furthest far-flung
Spiral of the stars,
Our paths were destined to be one –

As they waited, coiled and still, to be drawn
From the huge radiant skein
Of galaxies.

Within our separate labyrinths
The paths curved imperceptibly,
Circling closer, and closer still
To a goal unknown to us,

When, out of all the fragile strands
In the web of constellations,
Our two would finally entwine –

My soul's full circle
Mirrored in your eyes,
And all my branching paths
Converging in your limbs, your hands:

The shape of fate revealed
In the star of your body.

STARS

A chart drawn up
By an ancient hand,
Some dreamer looking out from land
To worlds of distant light
Across the dark sea of the sky:
His map, not for ships,
But for the mind to travel by.

RIVER

Still, as in the long
Soft light of summer, it gleams
In the mind of the forest
As it does in mine –
Coiling in and out of sight,
Stealthy, flashing, serpentine.

Along its banks
The densely woven trees
Stand mesmerized, deep roots
And mirrored branches reaching out
To draw their life
From its light,

As birds like arrows hunt among
The highest hazy leaves,
Then dive through liquid air to skim
The water's surface,
The river's wings
Rising to meet them.

There in the depths
Are fish made luminous
By the river's currents, the pulsing radiance
Of sun and swiftness
And the dark pools' languid,
Slow-revolving stillness

Where the coiled spirit lives,
Scales glinting in the shadows

As it gathers and extends
Its supple body –
Emerging from its glistening, transparent skin
Again and again.

STUMP

Deserted now, and sinking
Imperceptibly back into the forest floor,
It harbors still
The shadow of an ancient
Overarching tree, this ruin
Of a once formidable city.

Steeped in the soft light
Of leaves and lichen,
Moss drifts deep
On every terrace,
And brilliant fungi climb
The great steep stairways

Carved by some forgotten
Cliff-dwelling race.
How patiently they burrow
Into the dense, unyielding heartwood
Until finally it softens, and relents,
And opens a myriad

Dark mouths of mystery,
Where vision seekers once
Were planted deep
Within the fertile caves of dream.
Up on the heights, diviners
Search the sky for signs –

Cast themselves out
Among the leaf-lights, constellations
Of the deep green night,

Out along the branching pathways
Of the slow-spiralling heavens,
Into the brightness beyond.

There, they gaze into the hearts
Of stars that flash like birds
From limb to limb,
And follow with their nets
The butterfly whose iridescent wings
Hold both the dreamer and the dream.

Sometimes, strange visions trouble them.
Looking down upon their mountains'
Fearsome pinnacles and spires,
They see the remnants of a shorn-off trunk,
And hear a thunderous wind
Echoing among them.

They see their own world, like the mountains,
Rising, then worn away –
Consumed by the slow fire
Of centuries, the soft ash sifting down
In the last amber light
Of some future afternoon.

Then, the trees go on
Without them, the mosses
Cover their tracks.
Seedlings feed on the ruins.
The forest
Reclaims its own.

BOOK DESIGN & composition by John D. Berry and Jennifer Van West. The typeface is Minion multiple master, designed by Robert Slimbach as part of the Adobe Originals type library. Minion is based on typefaces of the later Renaissance, but is derived from no single source. Slimbach designed Minion in 1990, then expanded it in 1992 to become a multiple master font – the first to include a size axis for optical scaling. *Printed by McNaughton & Gunn.*